WHAT IS AN EMOTION?

Teresa Noto

What is an Emotion?
Illustrated and written

by Teresa Noto

www.Gihonbooks.com

info@gihonbooks.com

Hertfordshire, UK.

Contents

Dedications

Nanny,

I am so lucky to have had you as my Nan. I have never met nor will I ever meet anyone like you again. The only word for you is Nanny. You always told me to try. It only took thirty years, but I finally listened. Everything I have achieved in the last year is because of you. You are the reason I keep fighting.

I miss you everyday.

Mum,

thank you for your never ending support, and never losing faith in me, even when times were hard. You really are amazing. I am sorry for everything, and I am sorry I do not tell you just how wonderful you are.

Dedications

Denise Sheffield,

You are an exceptionally talented tutor, and by far an amazing person. You have gone above and beyond the call of any tutor or friend. You somehow got me through English. You helped me find my voice, and you have been a true friend, when I really needed to get away from it all. Your future students are extremely luckily to have you.

Ruth Dickson,

without you this book would not be getting published. You found me during a really hard and emotional time in my life. You have kept faith in me, which has given me the confidence I needed.

For

Nonna

Introduction
Nanny

Nanny was a kind, giving and loving person. Always thinking of others, but never herself. A bottle of polish and a cup of coffee never far away. So clean and tidy the dust was too scared to lay. Whatever she cooked it tasted like heaven. My Nan was superwoman and I'll tell you why: Years of suffering and brutal pain, yet never complained..., just carried on as if everything was ok. Many times she stared death in the face and each time she defeated death when others couldn't.

Nanny

Throughout the life she was given
she worked hard
in order to support her family.
Many would say she was truly amazing.

She was handed a hard and difficult life,
yet she never complained.
She continued to be a wonderful,
caring, kind, warm, welcoming
and loving person
who always put others first
even when she was unwell.

Nanny

This is a rare quality
in a human being to be so selfless.
Not a single bad bone in her body.
No matter how hard life got,
she kept fighting.
She never gave up.
She just kept going.

Nanny

There are no words
that can describe this true saint
who was sent by God himself
to teach us all how important
sharing true love is,
and the importance of caring
for one another.

A lot can be learned
from this woman
who only ever thought of others.

Nanny

We complain everyday
about how our lives could be better,
yet this someone who only ever knew
hardship, pain, and illness
never complained.
Just loved.

Introduction
Empty shell

Empty shell, You've reached boiling point with your emotions. You're giving up, even though you want to hang on. But there's nothing left to hang onto. You begin to feel you're losing yourself, becoming the living dead.

Empty Shell

An empty shell
filled with emotion,
falling upon itself
waiting to be rebuilt.
Filled with anger,
smashing to the ground,
waiting to put the pieces
back together.

Filled with love,
shot into pieces
hoping to be rescued.
Time proceeds.

Empty Shell

This shell begins to fade
into the darkness and loses faith.
The days turn into years,
this shell commences life once again, however
becomes soulless.

This empty shell
is filled with nothing,
unable to breath,
unable to occupy any
form of emotion,
as there is nothing left inside.
Just stone.

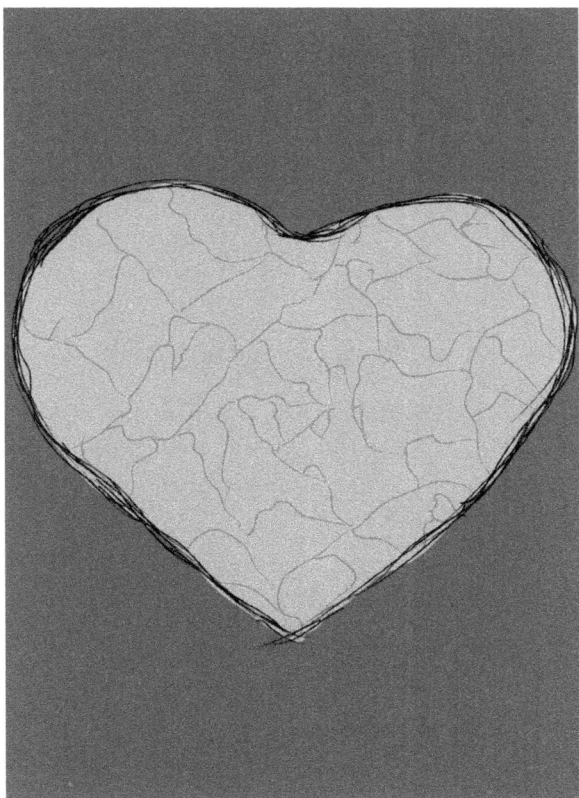

The force that
sets upon

The force that sets upon my heart
stops me from breathing,
as I feel its pressure closing in on me.

As it gets harder to breath,
I imagine the blade piercing my skin
gently releasing the pain within my heart.

I begin to wonder
if I let the blade in,
will it stop the pain?
Will it put an end
to all this madness within me?

The force that sets upon

As the force rips me wide open,
I imagine myself free.
I imagine the blade resting
softly letting the blood drip.
I imagine what it feels like
and for a moment I can breath.

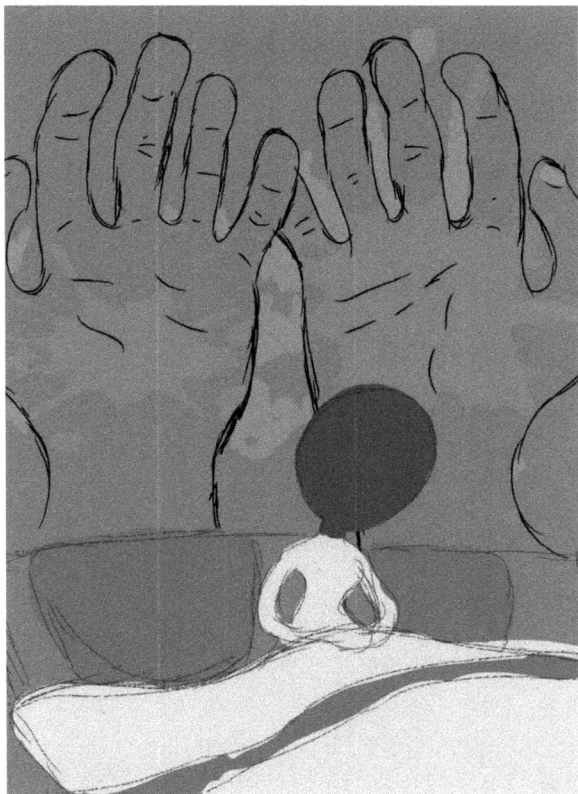

Glass box

I'm standing in a glass box.
I'm alone.
Banging my fists
against the glass screaming.
I try to feel an emotion,
but nothing will surface.

I keep screaming inside.
I'm screaming for someone
to help me.
Can you hear me?

Glass box

A sweet smell appears from nowhere.
Soon after I see a woman,
she's trying to help me.
The smell drives me crazy
as it gets stronger.

I begin to bang harder,
screaming even louder.
I'm so lonely.
I'm dying on the inside.

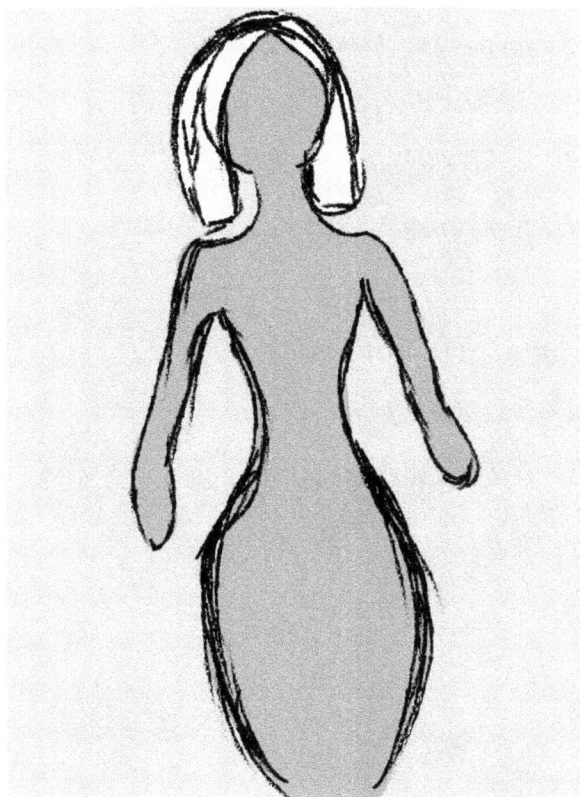

Glass box

Yet no one sees the pain I'm in,
no one sees this glass that surrounds me.
It's as if I'm not even there.
Even my friends pass me by.

Am I losing my mind?
Or have I masked this pain
so well that no one can see
through this glass that surrounds me?

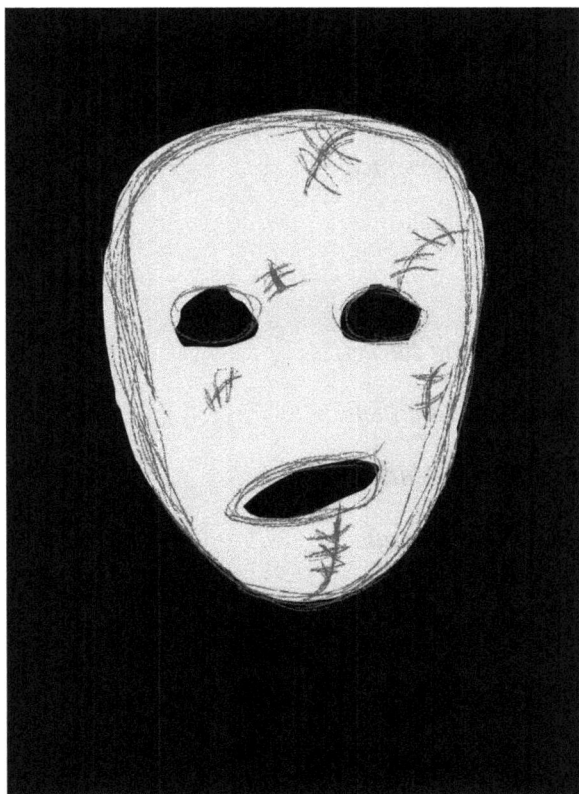

Glass box

Only this woman can see me,
but she can't break through.
I can't see her face,
just an outline.

I'm begging for help.
The signs are there,
but no one hears or sees me.
Only this woman.

Before I know it
this woman begins to fade away
leaving nothing behind
but the sweet smell of hope.

Then without warning
the woman is gone.
I'm left alone once again.
I'm left with nothing.
I am nothing.

Catch me

You keep striving to let yourself in
but you can't get though.
I try to open the door,
I freeze, I can't move.
I try to move my arm,
my hand, any part of me,
but nothing, I just stand there.

You try again this time,
kicking at the door.
I try again, but I'm motionless.

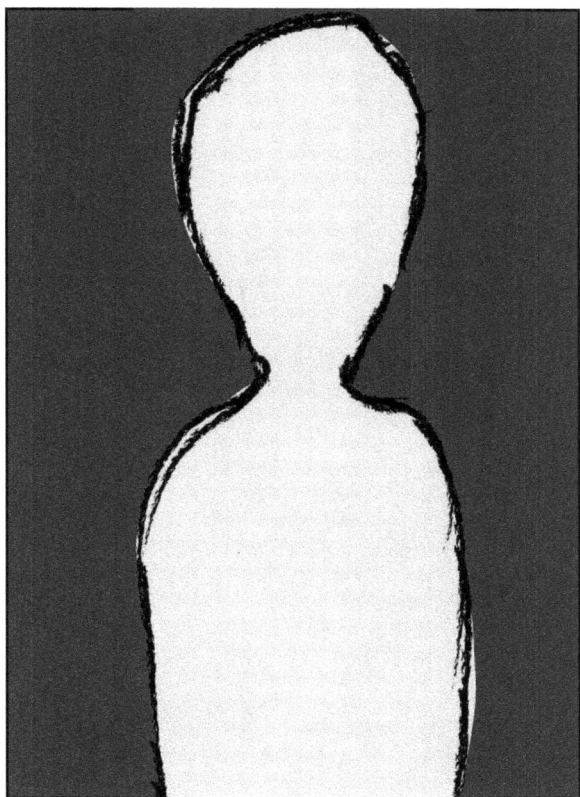

Catch me

You get louder.
I begin to panic.
I start to run.
I keep running.
I keep running as far as I can,
till I can't go any further.

You try chasing me.
I'm getting faster.
I tell myself to stop,
but I just can't stop myself.
The fear has court me.

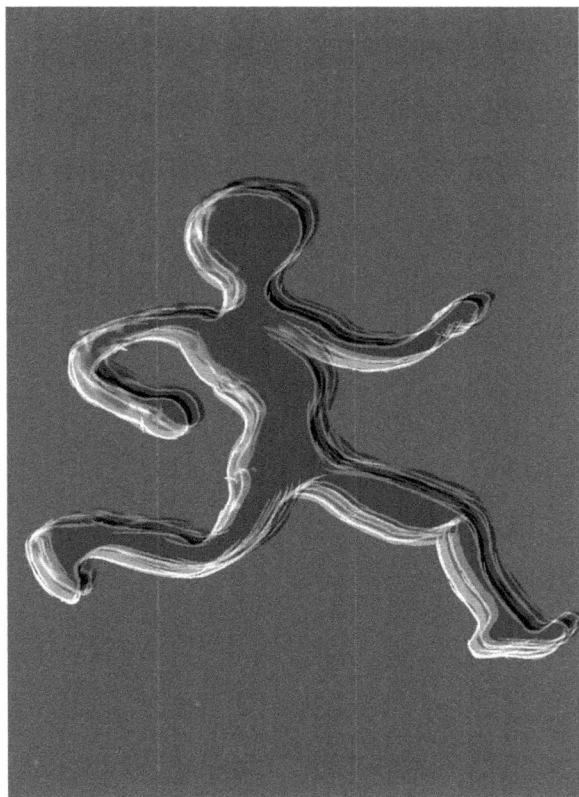

Introduction
Force you away

Unable to accept love. Run the moment someone gets to close. The pushing begins. In fear they will only leave, Just like everyone else has once they see the real me.

Force you away

I force you away
as you begin to rupture
though the cracks in my armour.
It's starting all over again.
The fear.
The running.
I don't even realise
I'm doing it once again.

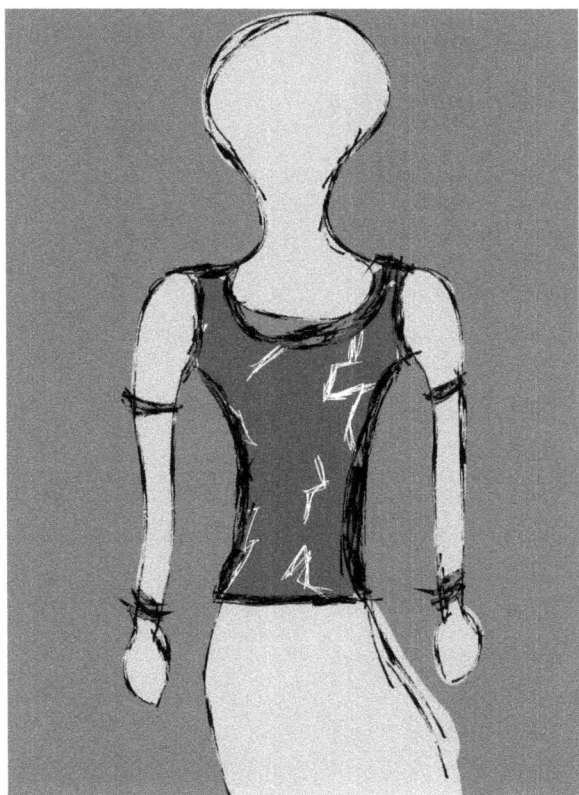

Force you away

I can't let her in.
I can't let anyone in.
I want to let her in,
but my inner demons
won't let me.

I keep pushing till there's
nothing left.
Can she hold on to me,
even with the madness
and chaos I bring?
Can she never let go?

49

Subject myself

Subject myself to the torture,
which lies within us all.
Overcome, the desire of letting go.
Open my eyes to the validity
that deprives us all,
never letting the lies of the world
blind me to the phony faith
that deprives us all,
never letting the false feeling of love
pierce my heart.

Subject myself

Subject myself to the loneliness;
I'm not the only one.
Overcome desires
that lie within my mind
blocking out the feelings
that blind my senses.
Open my eyes to the world,
only to deprive myself of happiness.
Give up on faith,
hope, and love just to be alone.

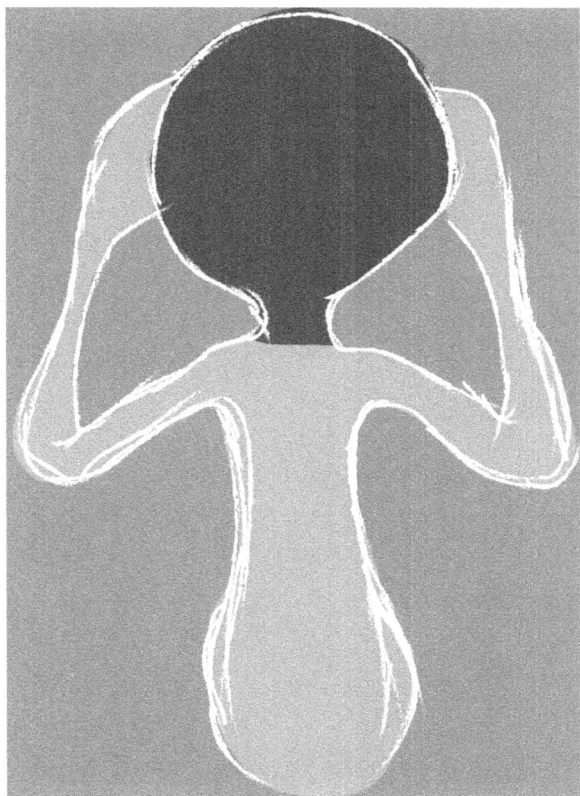

Pain

Pain is a meaningless cave with no feeling.
Loneliness seems to intensify on the inside.
It takes every part of me
it leaves me with no soul.

It hides in the darkness
it keeps me awake.
It leaves me with nothing.
It's taking over
every inch of my very being.

Pain

It holds me so tight,
I can't breathe.
My minds rushing
I can't focus on a single thing.

My eyes are turning black,
my skin becomes cold,
how am I still alive?

This pain that has no meaning
or reason is more alive than I'll ever be.
It grips me.

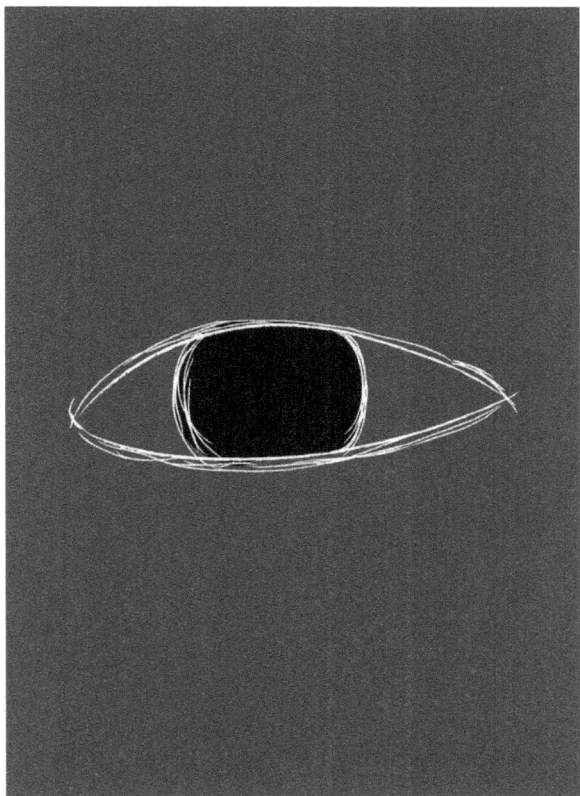

Pain

It's been here for so long,
I start to wonder
is it the pain that won't let go of me
or is it me that won't let go of the pain.

It's stronger than me.
It's the shadow
that walks beside me in the sunlight.
It holds my hand
when loneliness comes back to play.
It's every part of me.

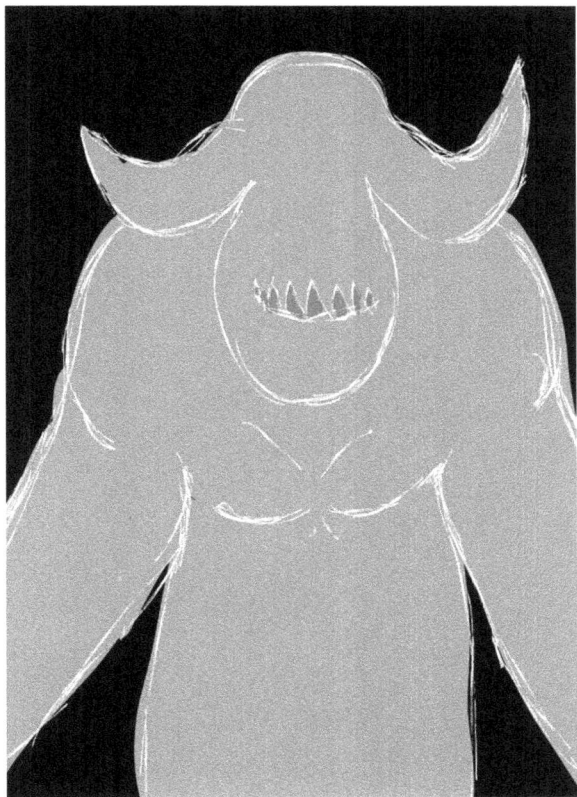

Pain

It's the words I speak,
it's the tone in my voice
it's the light in my eyes.
It's my everything.

Without pain, what else do I have,
I have nothing.

Cuts

I cut what's left of me
and give it to you.
So many pieces
have already been given,
I'm disappearing.

I cut myself in places no one sees,
to watch myself bleed.
I cut myself
to feel some kind of anything,
since it helps wash away the anguish.

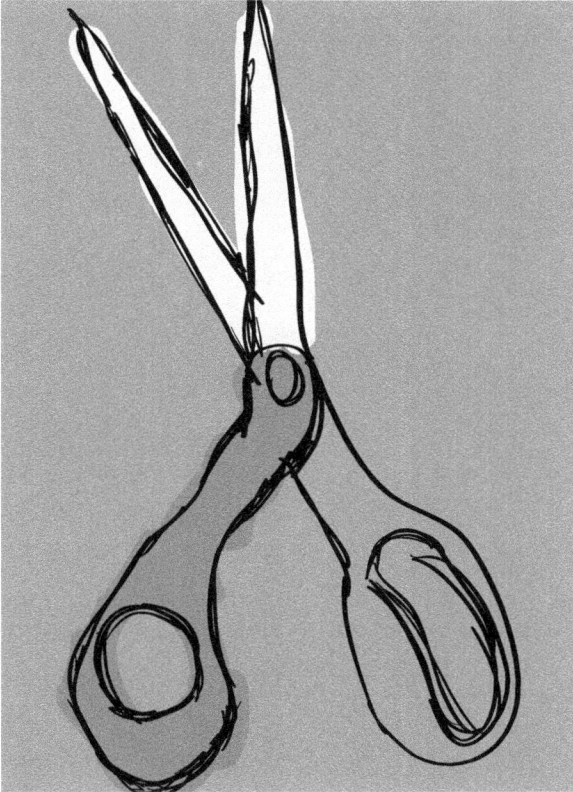

Cuts

The scars remind me
of what I have lost.
I cut myself because it's all I have,
it's the only thing I can turn to.
It's whom I cry to.

Dreaming

I'm dreaming for another place in time,
another me in another world,
another day where I can change it all.

I've fallen hundreds of times,
it doesn't get any easier.
This sorrow only gets deeper.
I feel like I'm fading away,
into the night of despair,
holding on to a dream
of finding a better day,
because this fear overpowers me,
leaving me lifeless unable to breath.

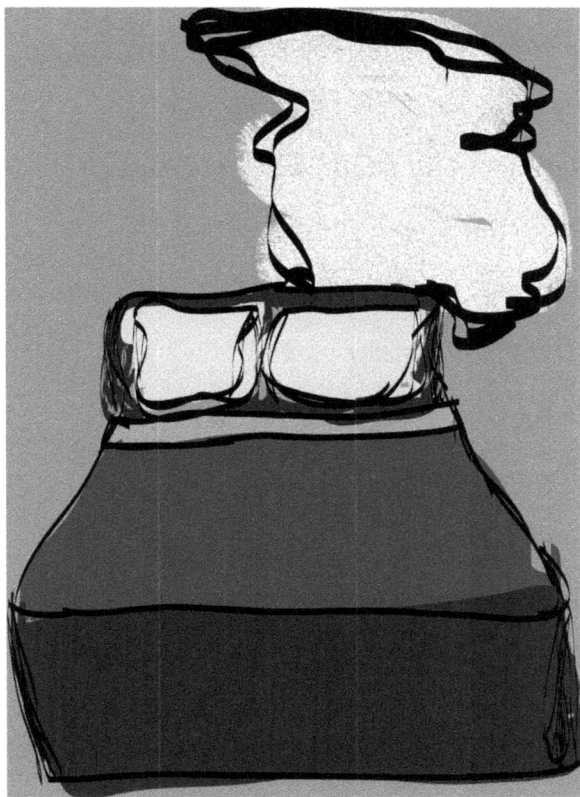

Dreaming

Dreaming just dreaming.
Hoping one day it will come true,
hoping it will finally happen to me,
me of all people, me.

But that day never comes.
I keep dreaming,
hoping, wishing
and praying
happiness will find me.

Letting go

I attempt letting go,
but the pain runs so deep
within my heart it won't release me.
It keeps me here in solitary
away from the world,
in some way keeping me safe.

I attempt to run away from it,
but I fall.
I scream until it hurts,
but no one hears me
through this barricade of pain.

Letting go

No one sees me,
I'm just a lie.
I hit the ground
and watch my hands bleed
hoping this is the end,
but it's keeping me alive.

I'll never be free from it
I'm too weak.
It's apart of me now,
I can't let it go.
I hold on to it.
Hoping it never leaves.

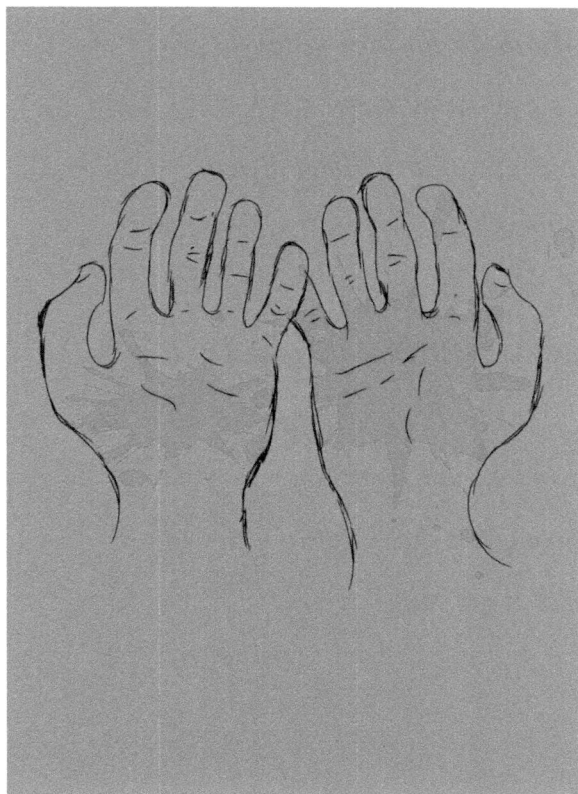

Understand myself

Words are far from between
as I lose it all again.
I can never understand myself;
I think too much,
I keep it all inside,
just to never show the pain I'm in.

I put a smile on my face every day,
hoping one day I'll believe myself
and it will all go away.

Understand myself

I can never understand myself,
I can never show myself
as the real me isn't likeable,
the real me isn't nice,
the real me,
I just don't know anymore.

I'm going nowhere fast,
I'm standing still
as everything flies by me,
is this really what life is?

Waiting

She sits there,
waiting in this small room,
full of odds and sods.
She doesn't really know
what she's waiting for.
She feels lonely,
unwanted and like her dream
will never come true.

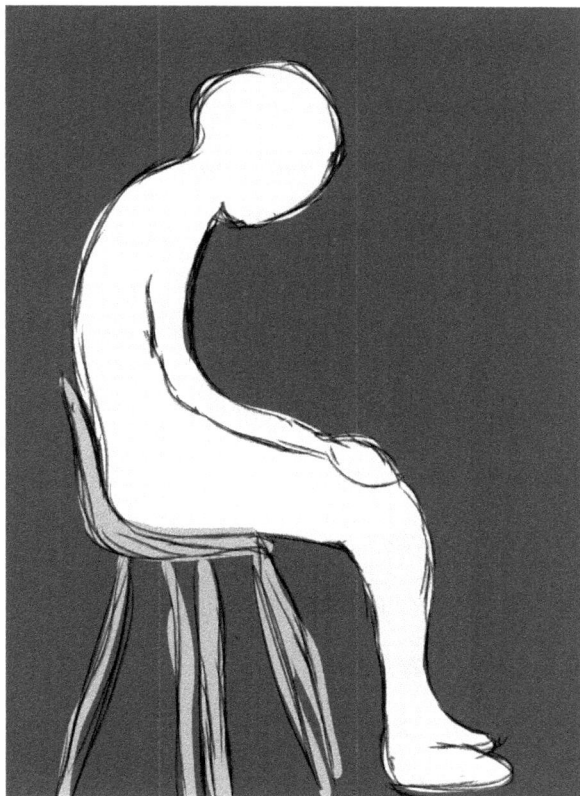

Waiting

She's unsure of herself.
Unsure of the life that has been given.
She remains waiting and calm.
What is it she's waiting for?
What is it she really wants?

Her thoughts are rushing at her
like a speeding bullet.
Her mind cannot keep track
of one thing to the next.
She tries to keep going
but her mind is giving up,
her mind is falling.

Waiting

Her heart can't seem to feel,
it seems to have given up too.
All she can do is run
through the emotions.
Nothing is real.

Time waits for no one
even more so for her.
Waiting, just waiting,
but for what?
Time, love or money?

Waiting

What is it an emotion to feel again?
Could it be trust even?
What is it she's waiting for?

Hope doesn't even seem to be there
it left a long time ago
along with love, trust, and emotions.
She tries to cry, but nothing,
just nothing.

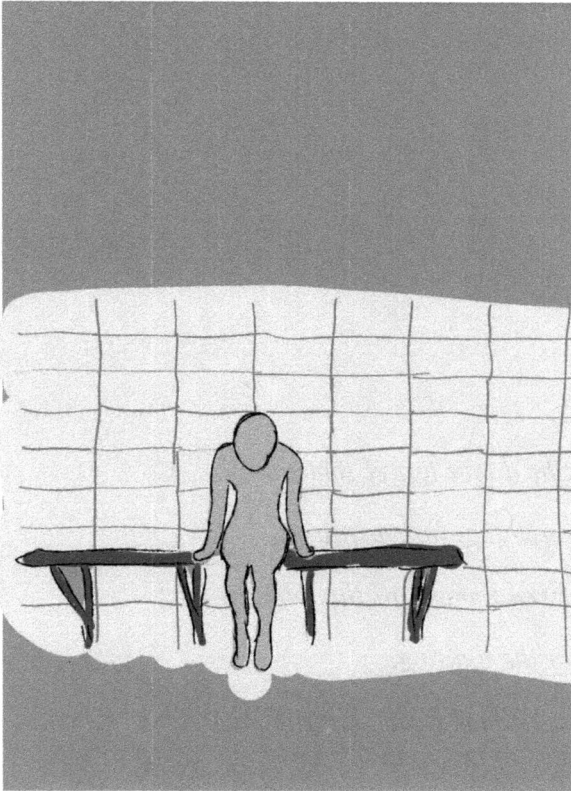

Waiting

She'd love to feel something,
anything, just anything.
Even though all this plays a part
in the waiting,
just what is she waiting for?

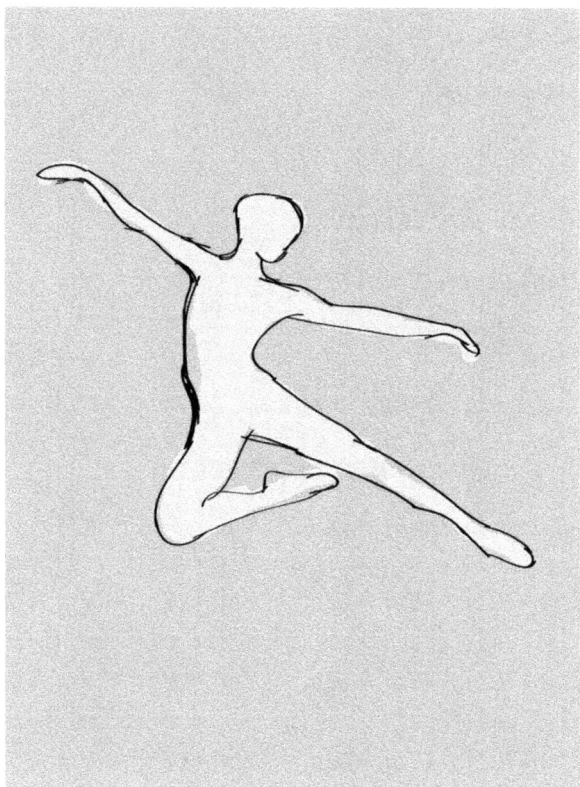

What is love but an emotion

What is love?
An emotion
we are governed to feel?
A pain that is given
and accepted willingly?

I ask myself this question.
Is it a thing that is just there,
just there in our minds?

What is love but an emotion

A program maybe?
Yes a program
that has been built into us all.

Maybe it is hope, the hope
that we are not meant to be alone
in this world,
that we are meant to be two,
not one.

Fear, maybe this is what love is,
a fear that we will die
with no one to care,
with no one to cry,
with no one to be sad,
with no one to show emotion
for a love they have lost.

What is love but an emotion

Some say it is a spark
between two people,
but where does this spark come from?
What even is this spark?
Is it bright lights that just appear?
Is it a feeling in your gut?

Just what is it?
Does love even exist?
Or is it just a false emotion
we are led to believe?

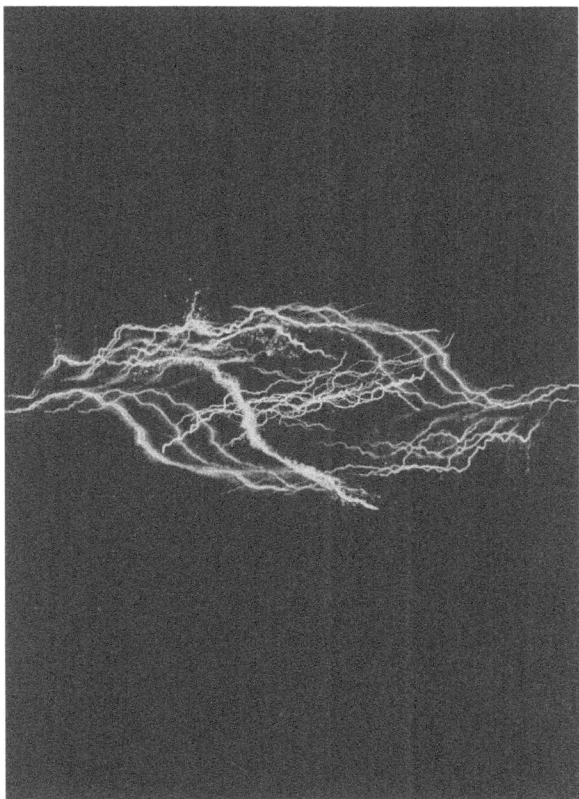

The force that sets upon 2

This road I have strolled upon
is soulless, an empty path
that has no end
only a dark lonely sky
that falls upon my lifeless self.

There is a force that sets upon
my heart that stops me breathing,
as I feel its pressure closing
in on me.
As it gets harder to breath
I imagine a gentle releasing
of the pain within my heart.

The force that sets upon 2

I begin to wonder
if I let this darkness in,
will it stop the pain?
Will it put an end to all this
madness within my empty soul?

As this force rips me wide open
I imagine myself free.
And for a moment, I can breath.

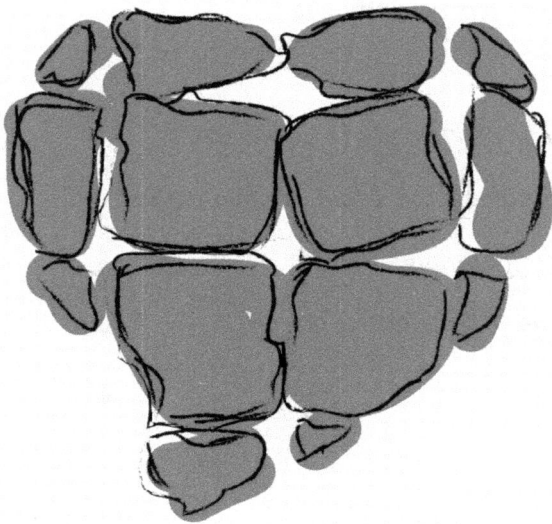

Freedom

Freedom. I miss that feeling.
The feeling of cold water
running down my body.
The purity it brought.

The carefree world of colours.
Peace. I wish I had freedom again.
To fly through the sky
and feel the air on my face.

Freedom

I wish I could go back
and stay within your arms.
Stay within what was once
thought of as love.
I miss being pure.

I miss the energy,
the connection I once had.
The freedom.
Being weightless, light,
true and open.

Introduction
I have never

What makes a man a Father? Can you call someone Dad, just because they helped create you? Can you forgive a so called Father, who was never there?

I have never

I have never once forgotten you.
I have never once forgiven you.
I've always tried to understand.
I've always hoped for an ending
to this never-ending story.

So many questions I wanted
to ask yet no answer can be given.
So many years have passed
with so much time wasted.

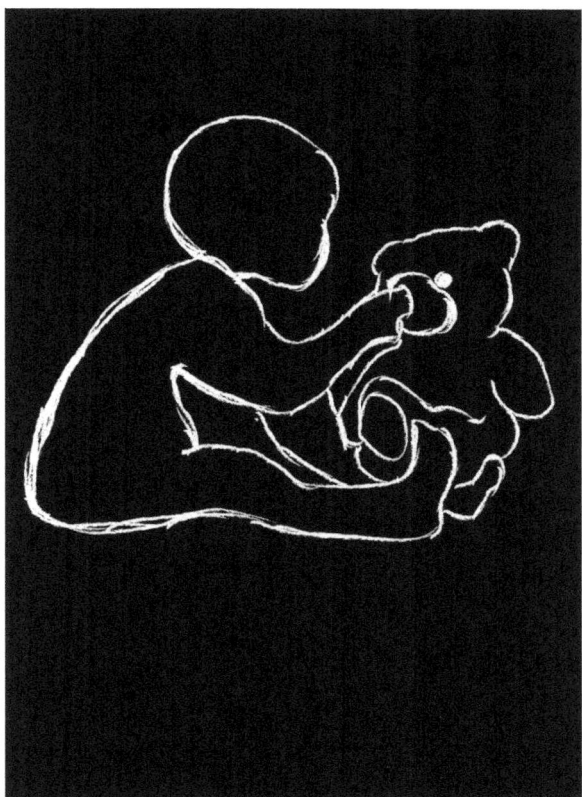

I have never

Now here before me
is nothing but lies.
I seek the truth.
I seek happiness.
I seek love.
I seek belonging.
But no answer can be given.

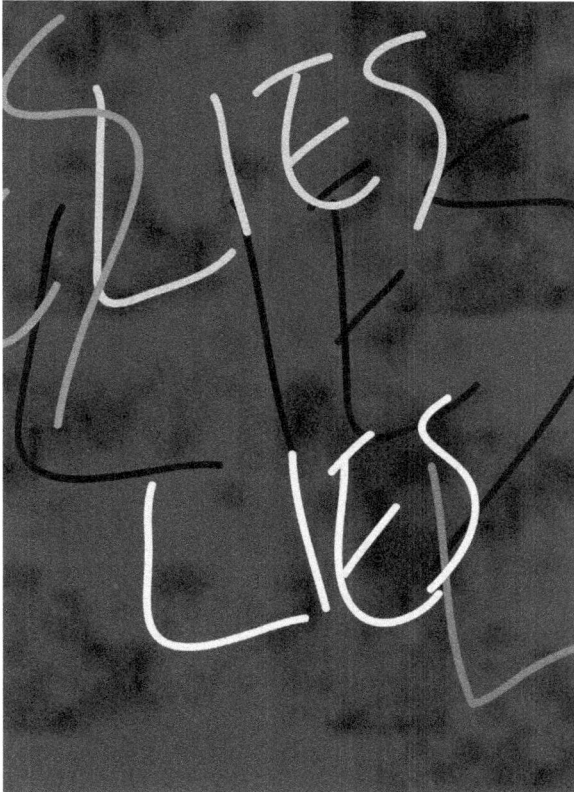

Blue eyes

Her eyes pull me in,
they are all I can focus on.
I can't walk away.
I try to listen,
but find myself staring into what appears to
be a little piece of Heaven.

Panic sets in,
whilst I feel my heart racing.
I merely try to speak,
only mumbled sounds
that resemble words come out.
What am I saying?

Blue eyes

I can't look at her,
in fear she'll see the truth
behind my eyes.
I look away
in an attempt to avoid her eyes.

They're so bright.
I'm losing myself in
her light.
I'm staring again.
I can't help myself
her eyes are keeping me
so absorbed.

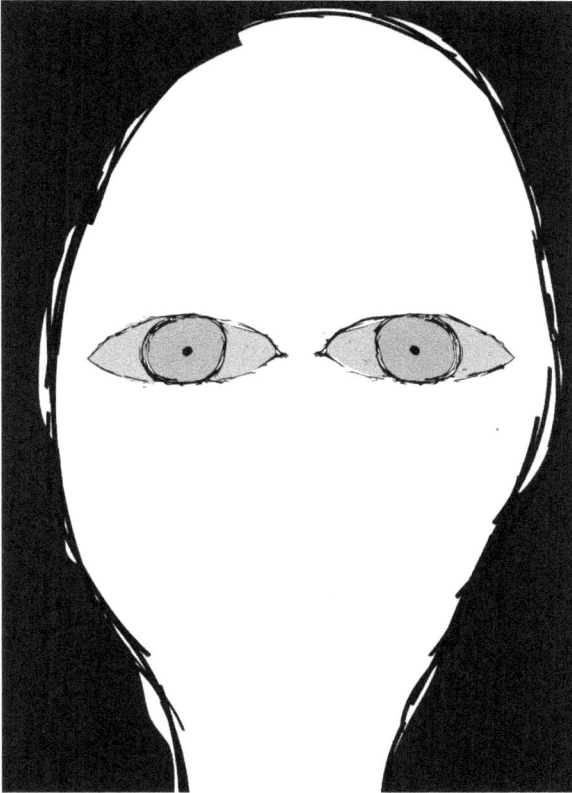

Blue eyes

I'm addicted.
Her lights taking over me,
her eyes are filling my soul
with the very thing that's missing.
I can't think,
I'm mesmerized.

Her eyes have captivated my soul to its very
core. The hold she has over me,
I can't say no.
I can't say anything, I just stare
and listen whilst I lose myself
in my own imagination.

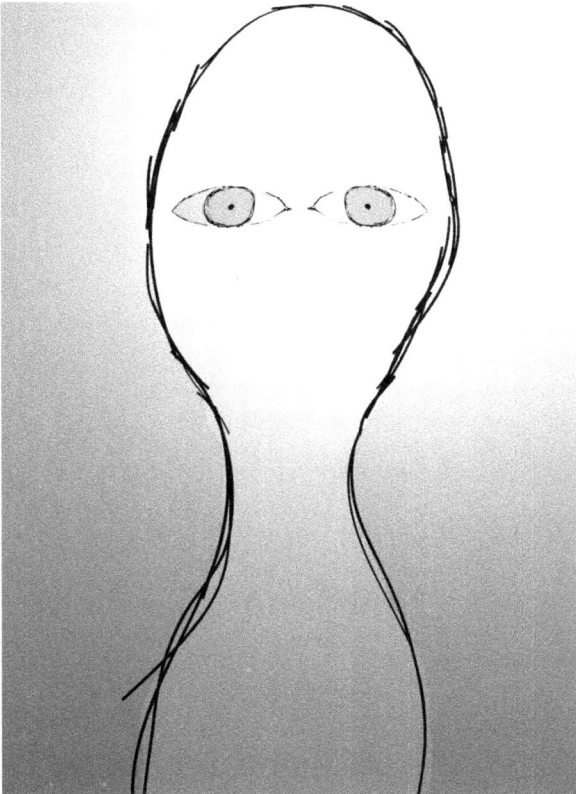

Younger me

I'm broken, torn, and lonely.
It has been this way for so long now,
I've forgotten what it means to be happy.
Am I a lost soul that's lost its way?
Have I suffered so much pain
that I can't be happy?

Is heartache my only friend?
There's no one here but me.
It's cold, black and lonely.
I'm calling out, but there's no reply.
I'm looking around, all I see is darkness.

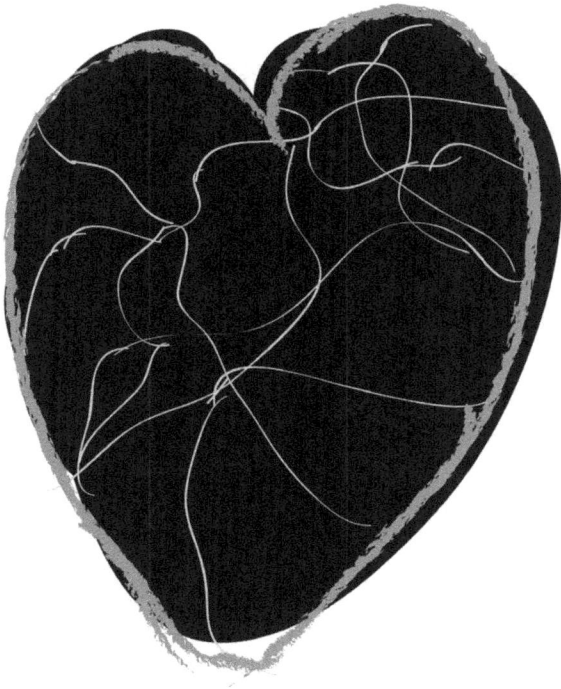

Younger me

I hear sounds of echoes.
I start walking
as the sensation of fear begins.
It's the fear of loneliness.
The further I walk,
the echoes get louder,
and images flash before me.

As I continue walking,
standing before me is a young girl.
I stop.
I'm gasping for air.
It's me.

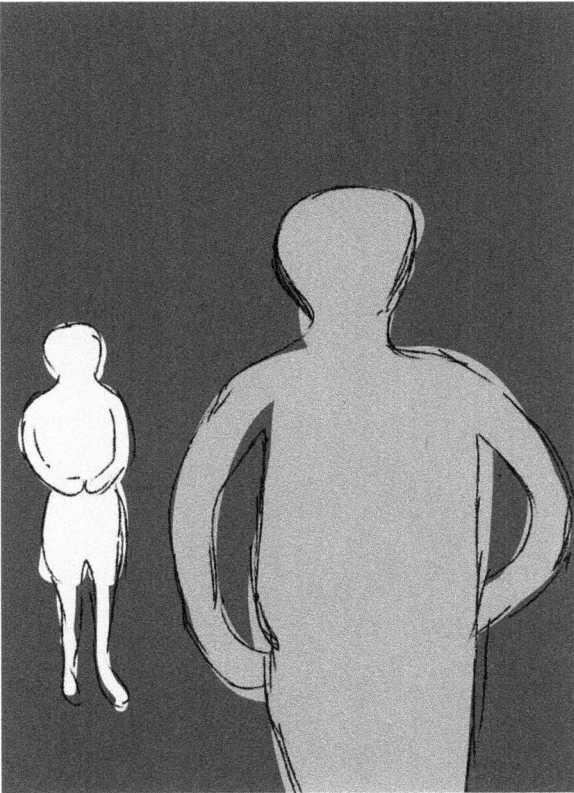

Younger me

I'm standing in front of myself.
She's happy.
She's smiling.
I try to go to her,
but she's surrounded by glass.
I want to reach out, but I cant.
I bang on the glass screaming.

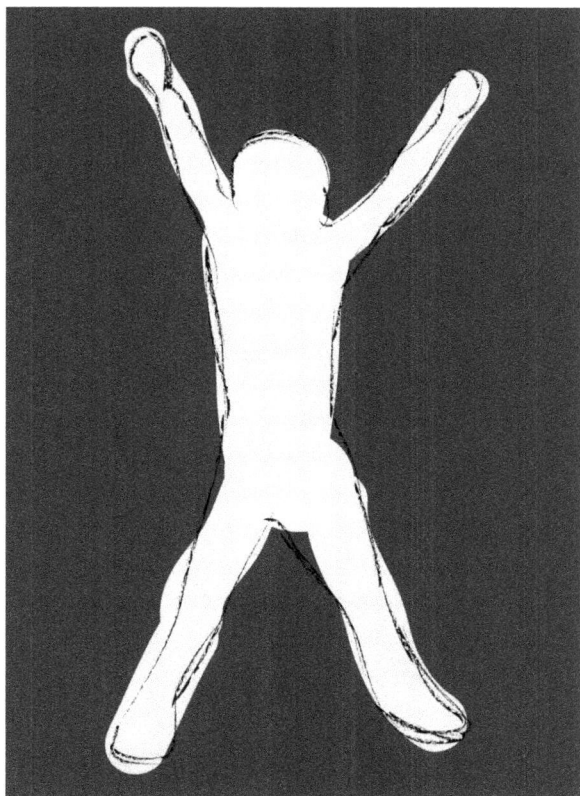

119

Younger me

She doesn't notice me.
I keep watching,
as this dark cloud appears.
Sensations of loneliness
and fear come back,
this time stronger than ever.

The younger me is crying.
I try to see why.
All I see is a dark black figure
standing over her.

Younger me

I'm banging and calling out,
but still nothing.
The dark black figure shows itself to me,
but only for second.
It's him, the reason for the fear
and the loneliness.

He begins to fade into the background
as her tears fall harder.
I hear her call out.
She's screaming.
She's screaming louder and louder.

123

Younger me

She's screaming out the name Daddy.
I'm left standing there watching.
The tears begin to fall.
I drop to the floor.

It's not real

It's not real.
It's only an illusion,
created by my own mind.
It's taunting me,
laughing as it gets closer.
It never leaves me,
It's always there surrounding me.

This fakeness that is me.
I can't be real.
I can't show myself.
No one understands,
What it's like.

It's not real

My mind won't leave me alone.
It keeps talking, talking, and talking.
I don't even know what I'm thinking.
Everyone always walks away.

They never stay.
They always leave.
No one cares.
I don't even care?

It's not real,
It's all in my head.
I never know what day it is,
from one day to the next.
They just all intertwine.
It's never ending,
this nightmare.

Birthday present

It's not the same.
Everything seems dead,
even silence.
Food has lost its taste.
I'm reminded of you.
The smell of coffee,
and polish haunt me.

I cry secretly,
when no one's watching.
I pray it's all a dream,
and I'll wake up soon.

I've shut myself off.
I can't feel anything.
I don't want to feel anything.
I can't describe this pain,
It's a mixture of everything.
I can't let you see me cry.
It's not what you wanted.

Birthday present

You had all my love,
I wish I had of told you.
The last moments we had
play over in my mind.
Images of suffering and pain.
There'll never leave me.

I'd do anything to hear you
say my name one last time.
I'd give anything to hear
your sweet loving voice
from the other room.

Its not the same without you.

Everything seems pointless,

and lifeless.

I want this to be over.

My heart can't take the pain anymore.

I'm broken.

You were my everything.

My shining light that kept me safe.

Birthday present

I know I'll wake up soon,
and hear the phone ring.
You'll be on the other end,
wishing me a happy birthday,
and this nightmare will end.

I keep telling myself to wake up.
Why can't I wake up?
I'm screaming on the inside,
praying, hoping you can hear me,
that anyone can hear me.
Why can't you hear me?
Why can't you wake me up?

Birthday present

It's nearly morning.
It's nearly time
for this pain to end.
I'd do anything to heal
the suffering that lies
within you.

I'm powerless.
I thought I was strong.
I thought I could do anything,
to keep you safe.
It's out of my control.

Birthday present

I'm struggling to breathe,
as I watch you lay there helpless.
I'm struggling to fight back the tears,
as you take your last breath.
This isn't a nightmare.
My phone isn't ringing.
I'm already awake.
But you're not saying happy birthday,
you're saying goodbye.

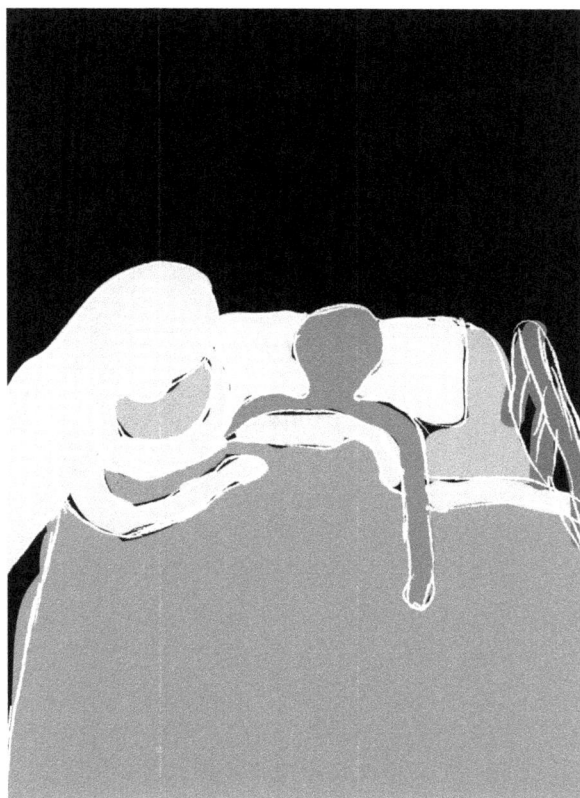

R.I.P

Nonna

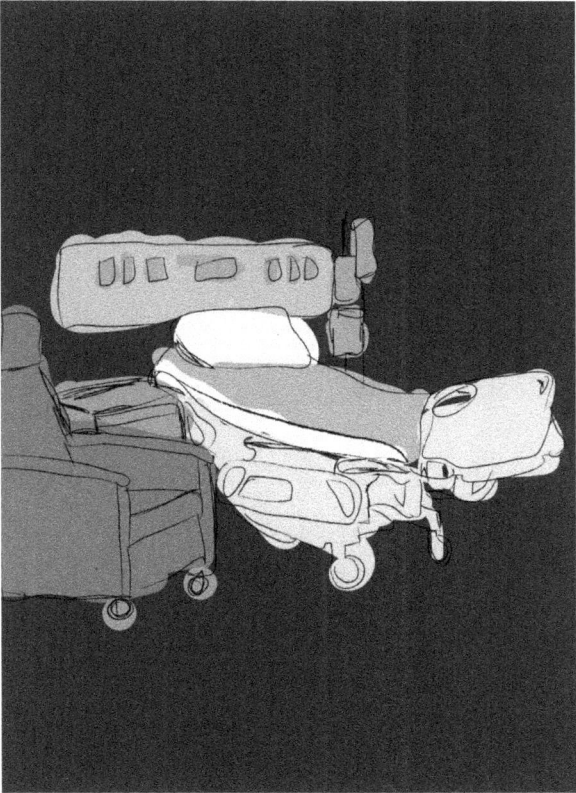

www.ingramcontent.com/pod-product-compliance
Lightning Source LLC
Chambersburg PA
CBHW070633030426
42337CB00020B/4000